September 27, 99

PORT DOUGLAS

REEF TO RAINFOREST COAST

PANOSCAPES

PETER LIK

WILDERNESS PRESS

Front cover - Four Mile Beach, Port Douglas
Back cover - St Mary's-by-the-sea, Port douglas

ISBN 1 876585 00 5

© **Wilderness Press** 1999 BK12

® **Panoscapes** is a registered trademark of Peter Lik's Wilderness Press Pty Ltd

Published by Wilderness Press, an imprint of Peter Lik's Wilderness Press Pty Ltd
PO Box 2529 Cairns Queensland 4870 Australia
Telephone: (07) 4031 3790 **Fax:** (07) 4031 3750
Email: info@peterlik.com.au **Website:** www.peterlik.com.au

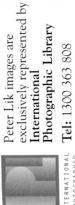

Peter Lik images are
exclusively represented by
**International
Photographic Library**
Tel: 1300 363 808
Fax: 1800 631 868

WILDERNESS PRESS
Peter Lik's Wilderness Press Pty Ltd

"My total dedication and
obsession with photography has
taken me on journeys into many
remarkable areas throughout
Australia. I captured this
collection of "Panoscapes" using a
specialist panoramic camera.
Because of the wider field of view,
this format enables me to portray
the true spirit of Australia on film.
Upon viewing these images I am
sure you will share with me the
tranquillity and solitude I
experienced whilst capturing
the stunning beauty of this
country."

*P*ort Douglas - village by the sea - is perhaps Queensland's most charming town. It is the closest town in Australia to the Great Barrier Reef and, at low tide, you can actually walk to the edge of the Great Barrier Reef from the palm-fringed beach.

The distinctive character and charm of Port Douglas is highlighted by many of its famous restaurants, shops, five star resorts and the beautiful Marina, where yachties share a yarn and tourists depart on luxury catamarans destined for the Great Barrier Reef.

On Sunday, hymns from St Mary's-by-the-Sea add atmosphere to the seaside market. Locals and tourists buy their favourite fresh tropical fruit and perhaps some local handcraft or a painting from the stalls.

The charm of this seaside village has been wonderfully preserved with nothing taller than a coconut palm.

Development is low-rise, low-key and relaxing. Boasting magnificent golfcourses, a wildlife habitat and popular Four Mile Beach lapped by the Coral Sea, Port Douglas is a hard place to leave.

From the village of Port Douglas, the Great Barrier Reef is just 8miles offshore affording excellent access. Further north, Mossman Gorge, surrounded by World Heritage Rainforest, offers cool refreshing swimming holes and breathtaking rainforest walks and hikes.

The thriving sugar town of Mossman, unaffected by tourism, still sees sugar trains run through the main street en route to the mill. Continuing north between sandy beaches and mist capped mountains is the Daintree. Surrounded by plantations of tropical fruit, tea, coffee and sugar, this is the real Queensland.

Port Douglas ... will you be charmed?

Coconut palms shade the hills of Port Douglas.

Previous page: Aerial view of the magnificent Agincourt Reef.

Charming St Mary's by the Sea overlooking Dicksons Inlet.

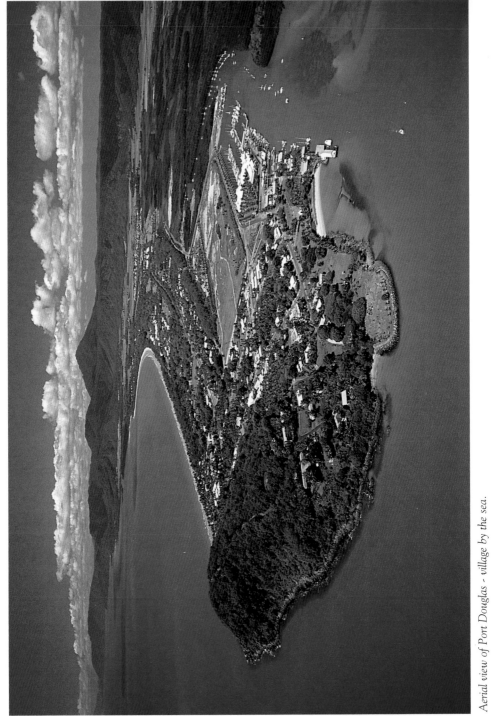

Aerial view of Port Douglas - village by the sea.

Four Mile Beach with the mountains rising from the Daintree in the background.

Port Douglas boasts some of the finest resorts in the world.

Next page: Port Douglas Marina provides the idyllic anchorage for any yachtie.

Exploring one of the natural wonders of the world - Agincourt Reef, off Port Douglas.

Underwater reef scene provides a mosaic of colour.

Four Mile Beach viewed from the lookout.

A cruise yacht heads out of Port Douglas for another day in paradise.

The distinctive character of the restaurants and bars which line Macrossan Street, Port Douglas.

Sunday markets in Anzac Park attract daytrippers and locals.

The Cook Highway north of Ellis Beach with Double Island in the background.

The road into Port Douglas fringed by tropical oil palms.

The Court House Hotel, Port's classic watering hole.

The colours of Port Douglas.

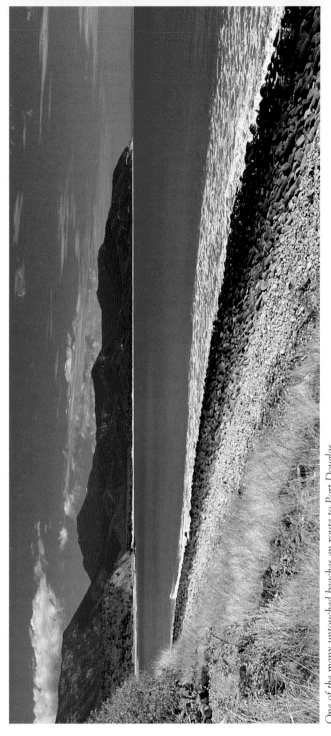

One of the many untouched beaches en route to Port Douglas.

Rex Lookout, halfway between Cairns and Port Douglas offers 180° views over the Coral Sea.

Abandoned cane cutters shack, Mossman.

Afternoon sun highlights a cane farmer's Queenslander cottage.

Sculptured sands at Yule Point.

Daybreak over the Coral Sea.

Above: Clownfish amongst anemone.

The Great Barrier Reef, one of the seven natural wonders of the world, embraces the shores of Port Douglas. Over 1500 species of tropical fish display their incandescent colors amongst thousands of varieties of coral.

Sundown over Ben Cropp's shipwreck museum.

Tranquil reflections inside Port Douglas harbour.

The Mossman River looking toward the rainforest clad Good Shepherd.

Previous page: Ancient World Heritage Rainforest at Mount Lewis.

Cool, clear waters at Mossman Gorge.

The Daintree River meanders through World Heritage Rainforest.

The Daintree River ferry crossing.

View north across canefields towards Port Douglas with Cape Tribulation in the background.

An aerial view of Mossman township.

Low Isles - a pristine coral atoll guarded by a classic lighthouse.

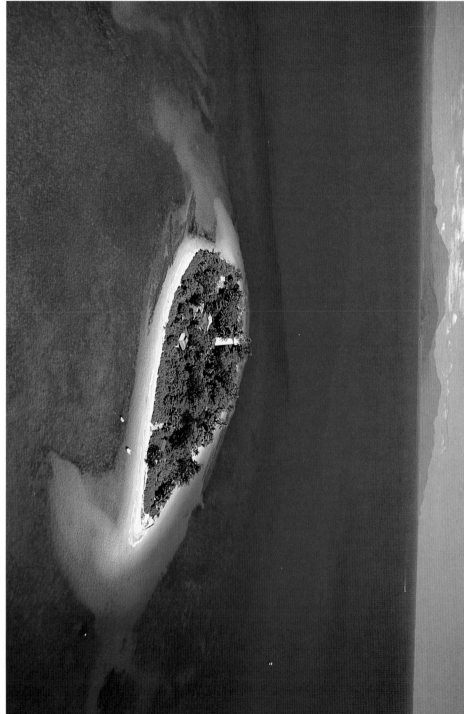

An aerial view of the Low Isles, Great Barrier Reef.

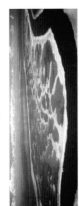